CW00642415

Historic Walks around Bleasdale

John Dixon & Jaana Järvinen

Historic Walks around Bleasdale
by John Dixon and Jaana Järvinen, 1988

Copyright © John Dixon and Jaana Järvinen, 1988

Published by Carnegie Press, 125 Woodplumpton Road, Cadley, Preston PR2 2LS

Typeset by Lloyd Williams, 22 Union Street, Southport

Printed by T. Snape & Co. Ltd., Boltons Court, Preston

First edition, February 1988

ISBN 0 948789 18 2

Contents

Introduction

Bleasdale rests in the south-west corner of the Forest of Bowland keeping a watchful eye over the plains of Amounderness. Overlooking, yet not actually in, the Fylde, Bleasdale stands apart from the rest of Lancashire, with a way of life and a rural character all of its own. As a local farmer once informed me, "You're not in Lancashire now lad, we have nowt to do with them. Up here's Bleasdale, it's bin that way since afore Roman times." Reference, no doubt, to the early settlements in these parts and farming families whose bloodlines go back to time immemorial.

Whichever way the Dale is approached, one does get the innate feeling of having crossed a boundary; the lanes seem more narrow, no villages as such, just small folds, isolated Post Offices, churches standing alone in fields, wayside chapels and lonely roadside inns. Your first visit to the Cross Keys Inn at Whitechapel will confirm for you these feelings on this delightfully neglected part of agrarian Lancashire.

The walks described here lead into Bleasdale from Longridge and Chipping, these being the nearest centres of population and on good bus routes. All the walks follow definitive public footpaths, though some of the stiles are missing in places. They are easy to follow, having been tried and tested by ourselves and friends. Lunch and refreshment stops are catered for in some surprising and comfortable settings. The walks avoid Beacon Fell Country Park, as we see nothing pleasurable in observing the different varieties of Ford and Datsun, Scots pines with assorted beer cans and crisp papers resting at their feet and groups of unfit motorists in garish attire that can be found in this nightmare of bureaucratic conservation. We hope that you thoroughly enjoy the walks, with their historical gleanings, and that Bleasdale is a district that you return to and get to know with a true affection time and time again.

Walk 1

Fellside to Dale Bottom

Approx. 3, 7 or 13 miles. Allow 2, 4 and 7 hours respectively.

O.S. maps SD 44/54 & 64/74 PATHFINDER SERIES.
Afternoon Tea: Bleasdale Post Office. Carry packed lunch and flask.
Start: Chipping (Corner Cafe)

This walk leaves Chipping to make an eastern approach on Parlick, then to descend on Bleasdale from the summit of Fair Snape Fell. After visiting the Bronze Age village, we wander back to Chipping, passing on the way many of the traditional 17th-century daleside farmsteads through some delightful rural aspects.

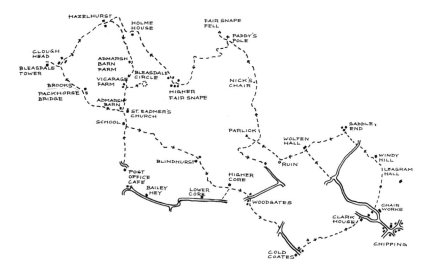

Looking at the map you will notice that the walk can be split into three or four smaller rambles, a handy thing if time is an important factor. The Post Office Cafe at Bleasdale affords a good starting point for visits to the Bronze Age village and Hazelhurst. With good lunches and teas, a car park and toilets, the cafe is a veritable oasis in this remote corner of Lancashire.

Chipping

The village of Chipping has a foundation which goes back to the Bronze Age. A burial mound was uncovered during road and building work to the north of the church in around 1770. An urn was revealed, marked with a lozenge decoration and

The Sun Inn, Chipping

into decay and only moss-land and the place-name of 'Wheatley' attest to its former 'golden' wealth.

containing fragments of bone. The site is remembered today by the name Grove Row, the site of the old Workhouse. The area acquired its status as a market place during the Roman period. Wheat, being the primary staple of the Roman army, was first cultivated in the newly cleared Vale of the Loud. This brought an age of prosperity to the district and a trading centre was soon established — horses, salt, lime, wheat and other grains being the major commodities exchanged. With the demise of Roman influence, the fields fell

TALBOT STREET, CHIPPING

Windy Street, Chipping, with Brabin's School House on the right

Today, Chipping is associated with the manufacture of chairs. This enterprise started in the mid 19th century, giving good business to local odd-job carpenters. One of these was John Berry, of Town End, whose dependants now run the thriving business at Kirk Mill, a company which produces over three thousand items of furniture each week — a long way from the odd-jobbers of a former age.

The village is still for the main laid out on its 17th-century plan and many of the original buildings stand today as strong and sturdy now as their builders intended. Those in Talbot Street and Windy Street are good examples.

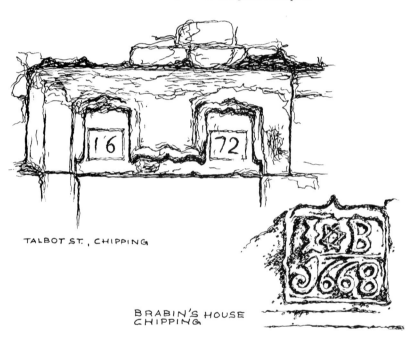

TALBOT ST., CHIPPING

BRABIN'S HOUSE
CHIPPING

John Brabin's School House

The inscription above the door of the school reads: "THIS SCHOOLE FOUNDED BY JOHN BRABBIN [sic], GENTLEMAN, DOCE DISCE VEL DISCEDE 1684. C.P.*R.P.*I.H.*R.M." — the latter being the initials of Christopher and Robert Parkinson, John Haythornthwaite and Richard Marsden.

Brabin was a local dyer and cloth merchant who acquired his wealth through the 'putting-out system' of manufacture. In his will of April 1683, he granted monies for the establishing of a school in the village. This grant also provided for the uniforms of sixteen pupils, shelter for the local poor through the building of almshouses and the cost of three boys to be apprenticed to a trade annually.

John Brabin's House stands in Talbot Street, next to the post office. The doorhead bears the date 1668 and an inscription reads: "LET HIM THAT LOVETH GOD LOVE HIS BROTHER ALSO".

CHIPPING

St. Bartholomew's Church, Chipping

A church was established here some time before 1230, but little is known of the early foundation. For the most part the present fabric of the church represents the major restoration of 1873 but a few interesting pieces remain from former ages. The oldest of these is a cross base which stands next to a 16th-century chest of Belgian origin. This base lost its position and shaft some time after 1610, probably during the Commonwealth period. A 14th-century piscina can be found in a recess in the south wall of the sanctuary. The font is by far the church's finest piece. It dates from 1520, supposedly the gift of Bradley of Bradley Hall, whose initials appear on one of the shields. The devices on the other shields represent the instruments of the Passion: the nails, the hammer, the pincers and the scourges. There are two blank shields whose designs have been obliterated; these were possibly the five wounds of Christ and the Sacred Heart. Around the base are the inverted letters A M G P D T — Ave Maria Gratia Piena Dominus Tecum (St. Luke. Ch.I. Verse 28).

Outside, in the churchyard, stands a sundial upon stone steps with the date 1708 and the initials of the churchwardens of the time. In the church porch can be found the initials of John Parkinson of Coldcoates, along with the date of his death, 1771.

Chipping to Wolfen Hall

Walk down lane at side of corner cafe, past the church tower and on to fork in lane. Go right and walk down, passing chair works and Grove Square and up to go over stile on driveway opposite mill lodge. Follow right-hand fence up to go over stile. Follow the hollow-way on, passing mounds, to go over stile in fence. Follow path to corner in wood and down to go over footbridge. Walk straight up to enter farm lane on left of house. Follow lane down and up to go through gate onto road. Pass through gate opposite and walk up to Saddle End to go left at cable post at farm entrance. Follow right-hand fence around the small wood to pass through gateway in fence. Follow left-hand fence, veering right to go through gate straight ahead. Walk directly across the field and follow path down to go over footbridge and follow path up to go over fence stile by gate. On, through gate on left, to follow right-hand fence on, through gateway, and on into farmyard via gate on right.

Wolfen Hall

Wolfen Hall

Wolfen Hall, or Wolf House as it was formerly known, was once the old manor house of Chipping, being the home of John de Knoll of Chippindale and later passing by marriage to Roger, third son of Robert Shireburn of Stonyhurst. The Shireburns, along with the Hoghton family, became the largest landowners in the district, both holding rival courts in the village. In St. Bartholomew's Church there was the Shireburn Chantry, also called Wolfhouse Quire. This was founded in 1519 by Roger Shireburn and used as a burial place for the Shireburns up till the late 17th century.

Wolfen Hall stands above the village at the bottom of Wolf Fell, overlooking Longridge Fell and the Vale of the Loud. The house is well maintained, giving a solid foreground to the backdrop of the fells.

Wolfen Hall to Parlick & Fair Snape Fell

Pass front of house, over cattle grid, then walk up the field on a slight right diagonal to pass through gateway in wall and on to ruin up ahead. At the ruin go over the stile on right then down to cross the stream. Walk up the hill to the summit of Parlick Pike. Follow the path along the ridge, passing Nick's Chair, to Paddy's Pole Cairn on the summit of Fair Snape Fell.

Parlick Pike

Parlick Pike is first mentioned in 1228 as 'Pirloc', a name that could have a pre-Celtic derivation. The second element 'lick' comes from the Old Norse word 'lykkja' meaning 'a loop' — Parlick does 'loop' off Fair Snape and Saddle Fell, as can be clearly seen from any map. Could it be 'pear loop'?, again, the pear emphasises the 'loop' shape.

Parlick has always been a rallying point for local Catholics, especially during the Jacobite Rebellions of the 18th century. Tales are told of lights burning on the summit at the very dead of night, where men would set their plans against the Hanoverians. Today the Pike is a rallying point for hand-gliding enthusiasts who play on the thermals that rise up from the valley between here and Saddle Fell.

Fair Snape Fell to Higher Fair Snape Farm

From the wall shelter walk past the cairn to find the path leading

Higher Fair Snape

down the fell. Zig zag your way down to go through gate in wall, and follow the track down to Higher Fair Snape Farm.

Higher Fair Snape

HIGHER FAIR SNAPE

HOLME HOUSE

The land around Fair Snape is a true reflection of its old vaccary name — the beautiful pasture — and sitting above this delightful aspect are the two 17th-century farmsteads that make up Higher Fair Snape. This was the original home of the Bleasdale line of the Parkinson family and a tablet above the main house doorway bears the family coat of arms, with the date 1637 and the initials of Ralph Parkinson. The second house was built after land next to Fair Snape Fell was divided between the Parkinsons and their relatives the Richardsons. The two families quarrelled often, especially about rights of common pasture at Admarsh and the grinding of corn at Brock Mill. The former involved several families hereabouts, finally requiring the Crown to sort things out.

Higher Fair Snape Farm to Holme House

Looking at the coat of arms on the house, go left and along trackway by side of barn, through gate and through gate on right of barn. Walk along the cobbled track, through gate, and on, through gate to follow stream down to go over slab-bridge two thirds of the way down. Follow brook down to go through gateway. Follow right-hand fence to trackway, right, and follow trackway on, through gate and on to enter Holme House farmyard by gate.

Holme House

In 1798 Richard Parkinson of Hazelhurst left Holme House to his second son, John, who married Margaret Rhodes of Thornley. Their initials and the date, 1802, can be seen above the front doorway of the house. In the front garden stands an attractive sun-dial along with the weight of an ancient cheese press.

Holme House to Hazelhurst

Walk past the house and follow lane to Hazelhurst.

Hazelhurst

A hamlet known as Coolan once existed here, consisting of six cottages, the inhabitants making a living from wool combing and straw hat manufacture. Only the old village stocks and a deserted cottage remain today as forlorn reminders of their industrious enterprise. The wool was transported as far as Burnley and Halifax and the packhorse bridge was built along the route at Brooks. Careful inspection of the farm walls around Hazelhurst will reveal the remains of mullioned windows, dressed building stone and old doorheads, again part of the old Coolan.

HAZELHURST (COOLAN).

The earliest record of the Parkinsons living here is in 1562. In 1842, Robert Parkinson Jnr. sold the estate to William Garnett, the builder of Bleasdale Tower.

Hazelhurst to Admarsh Barn

On leaving Hazelhurst turn right after group of trees. Follow edge of trees down to go through gateway in remains of stone wall (pieces of mullions are to be found in the wall). Walk down on a left diagonal to go over stile by the gate in the fence. Cross field on a slight left diagonal to go over stile and footbridges in far corner. Follow track to go through gate and on up to go over stile by gate. Walk on to go through gate into farm lane. Left and walk down to Vicarage Farm (ask here for permission to visit Bronze Age village). Follow lane down to St. Eadmer's and Admarsh Barn.

St. Eadmer's Church

The true origins of this chapel are lost in the pages of history. The first mention of 'Eadmor's chapel' is on a 1598 map of Lancashire. In 1610 it was described as 'a chapel without service in the king's chase' and the stipend was said to be detained

by Robert Parkinson, commissary of Richmond. In 1689 Richard White of Chipping had the Bishop of Chester's licence to preach in Admarsh Chapel and in 1702 Christopher Parkinson of Hazelhurst gave £5 10s a year for the wages of a minister. Because the name Admarsh was thought to be connected with the historian of that time St. Eadmer, friend of St. Anselm, Archbishop of Canterbury during the reign of William Rufus, the church was renamed St. Eadmer when it was rebuilt in 1835.

St. Eadmer's

Windows from the Elizabethan chapel can be seen today built into the fabric of the tower and the wall to the right of the churchyard gate contains decorated stones from the original building.

Admarsh Barn

Admarsh Barn stands opposite the church, aside the old lane down to Brooks. The doorhead of the barn is dated 1720 and bears the initials of Robert Parkinson. When the adjoining lands were enclosed in 1548 the Admarsh district remained as a common pasture and turbury, where turf was collected for fuel. In 1591 the Queen was asked to divide the common pasture as it was stated to be abused by some of the inhabitants.

William Norris resided at Admarsh Barn Farm in 1813, then known as the Parkinson Charity Farm. The present house bears the date 1814.

ADMARSH BARN

Admarsh Barn to Brooks Packhorse Bridge

Follow the trackway from the barn down to Bleasdale Tower driveway. Turn right and walk down to Brooks.

Brooks Packhorse Bridge

The bridge was built for pack-horses transporting the raw and finished wool to and from Coolan to the Pennine manufacturing areas. The bridge was erected in the mid 19th century on the site of the old river ford. The old trackway was 'lost' when a private road and bridge were built by the Garnetts of Bleasdale Tower.

Brooks to Clough Head Bridge & Hazelhurst

Walk on up the roadway, into the wooded driveway, to go right at Clough Head cottages, on down to the bridge. Carry on up the trackway to Hazelhurst.

Clough Head Bridge

This bridge was built by the boys of North Lancashire Reformatory School at Clough Head between 1858 and 1859 under the guidance of Christopher Foster, mason instructor at the school. Above the upstream arch of the bridge is a dated foundation stone and above the downstream arch is a carved tablet showing the bridge's tools of construction. The school was established by W.G. Garnett J.P. of Bleasdale Tower in 1857, to give one hundred boys useful employment, principally in agricultural labour, and their farming operations brought many areas of moorland into good cultivation.

Clough Head Bridge

Vicarage Farm to Bleasdale Circle

On leaving Vicarage Farm enter the field on the left by gate to follow left-hand fence to go over a stile. Walk across the field on a slight left diagonal to enter the wood by a stile. Walk on in the wood to find the Circle. Retrace your steps to farm lane.

Bleasdale Circle   SD 577460

This complex post-and-stake circle monument was discovered and partially excavated in 1898/9 and later re-excavated in 1933/5. The site was seen to comprise of a circular mound, 11m in diameter and 1m high, surrounded by a single-causewayed ditch floored with birch poles 10 to 20cm in width. Originally these would have been in the form of woven hurdles. Eleven large oak posts (their position now marked by concrete pillars) formed a circle upon the mound, with an avenue of three poles on each side across the east facing causeway. In the centre of the mound, at a depth of 56cm, was a stone lined cist containing two inverted cremation urns. One of the urns held a pygmy or 'incense' cup. The above circular feature is surrounded by a 60m diameter palisade consisting of twenty-two large oak poles 8m apart, between which were smaller posts. The outer circle has an entrance on the south east and what could have been a double gateway at the eastern end of the avenue. A number of burned circular patches of soil were found within the outer circle. These were around 3-4m in diameter, suggesting living huts destroyed by fire. These huts are assumed to be of a type consisting of a central pole, roofed with thatch with stone or earthen walls plastered with cow dung and clay over a slightly excavated round pit.

The cinerary urns were 21cm in height, made from local clay mixed with coarse sand. A radiocarbon date of 1810±90 BC (NPL-69), was obtained from timber recovered from the inner circle. If this date is correct, the well developed Pennine urns recovered from the cist are amongst the earliest collared urns to be found in Britain.

To conclude, what we have at Bleasdale is an Early Bronze Age II circular village site with an off-centred communal hut, surrounded by a ditch, outside of which would be several living or mating huts. The whole was enclosed within a palisade of oak pole construction.

Bleasdale Circle

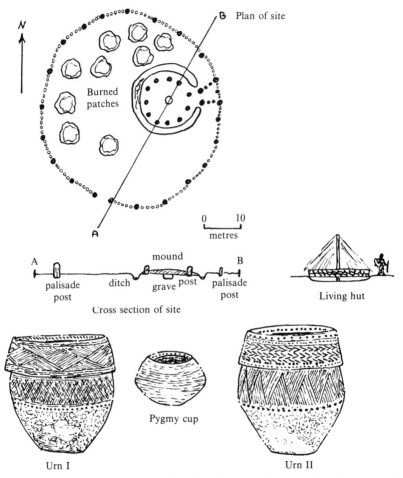

An identical site to that of Bleasdale has recently been identified east of Chipping at Fair Oak Farm and, along with other Bronze Age activity in the surrounding area, it all seems to point to the settled nature of society during the Bronze Age in the region.

Those returning to Chipping should now follow the directions to Blindhurst, but if lunch is desired then follow the lane down, past the church and school to the Post Office Cafe. What follows now is a description of Higher Brock Mill, Bailey Hey and Lower Core, which all stand beside the roadway between Woodgates and the post office.

Higher Brock Mill

The post office and cafe were once the blacksmith's forge situated just down the way from Higher Brock Mill. The mill was built by Anthony Richardson (second husband of the widow of Richard Parkinson). Ralph Parkinson refused to acknowledge the owner's right of soke, as it was a newly established mill. He in turn was refused the right to grind his corn.

Bailey Hey

Bailey Hey used to be an inn known as 'The Dog and Partridge' for a considerable time; why it was abandoned is not known. Thomas Parkinson, churchwarden at Goosnargh church, resided at Bailey Hey in the 1720s.

A flight of stone steps at the front of the house leads up to the old lodging room

used by the packhorse drovers. Lime was brought from Clitheroe and wool taken back and on to Halifax. The old name for these ponies was 'Lime Gals' — Galloway Ponies. The rear of the house still displays some of its ancient mullioned windows and at the front several hood mouldings frame the central portion windows.

Bailey Hey

Lower Core

Today Lower Core is just a 19th-century farmhouse but a stone built into the doorway of one of the farm buildings recalls the earlier farm house building. It has the date 1661, with the initials J.L. (Lowdes of Mitton). Inside the present house is a picture which, given the ancient mullions and the background view, could very well be that of the old building.

LOWER CORE

The place-name 'Core', first recorded in 1228 as Couere, is an old name for Parlick Pike — meaning a 'hood' or 'cap', from the Old Norse 'kofri'.

St. Eadmer's to Blindhurst

Walk down, past the school, to go over cattle grid and into field on left to follow left-hand fence to go over stile by edge of wood. Go through wood heading slightly right to go over stile. Cross the field on a slight right diagonal to go through gateway. Walk on to lane and along to cattle-grid to go right following left-hand fence and brook, on to go over footbridge and through gateway. Walk upstream to edge of trees and on up to go through gateway in front of you. Walk on, then follow left-hand fence up to go through gate. Follow track up to enter farmyard by two gates. Pass barn and house (steps of a spiral staircase built into the wall on right) then through gate and around to front of house.

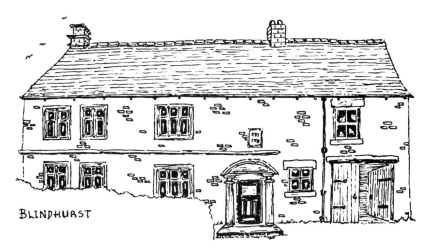

BLINDHURST

Blindhurst

Blindhurst presents an interesting frontage, with its mullioned and transomed windows and the pillared Georgian doorway, all reflecting the wealth of its builder, Richard Edward Parkinson, whose initials appear on a tablet above the doorway with the date 1731. Christopher Parkinson of Blindhurst, eldest son of Edmund (died 1607), succeeded the main moiety of the estate and was chosen as deputy Steward of the Forest of Bowland in 1611, under the Parkers of Browsholme.

Antony Parkinson of Blindhurst (1666-1728) joined the Franciscans at Douay, taking the name Cuthbert and thus forgoing his rights of inheritance of Blindhurst, and was sent on the English Mission in 1695. As well as being a missionary he became a Franciscan historian, his *Collectanea Anglo-Minoriticain* being published in 1726. He went on to become Provincial of the Order.

The rear of the house has mullioned windows and built into the corner of the

barn wall are steps from a spiral staircase, re-used as quoins. Inside the house is a fine corbelled mantelpiece and corner cupboard.

The place-name Blindhurst means 'a dark or obscure wood', recalling the forest of long ago.

BLINDHURST

Blindhurst to Higher Core

Walk down farm lane, over cattle-grid and directly on across field to go over stile in small section of walling. Follow left-hand fence to go over foot-bridge. Walk on up the hill following left-hand fence to gateway (do not go through). Walk around and follow left-hand fence up and along wall in front of house to go over fence into farmyard.

HIGHER CORE

Higher Core

The present farmhouse was built in 1731 for Edmund and Margaret Parkinson. The original house of around 1600 now forms part of the barn and is a listed building. Careful observation will reveal the old low mullioned windows and other features of that time. In the front garden of the farmhouse is the weight of an old cheese press and the headstone from a 17th-century fireplace.

Higher Core to Woodgates

On leaving farm, go round farmbuilding on left to find stone wall (notice weight of cheese-press) and follow wall to corner. Cross field directly to go over stile in wall. Follow left-hand hedge to go over stile down to roadway. Cross road and walk up Woodgates driveway to front of house.

Woodgates

Woodgates, formerly Wood Yate, has a rather forceful inscription upon its datestone. It reads: "Richard and Catherine Parkinson. 1768. Jubeoprofanos hinc a befse" — freely translated: "I order all unrighteous persons to keep away from here". Obviously a couple with strong religious convictions, who later gave birth to one Richard, who went on to become Canon Richard Parkinson who numbered Charles Dickens as one of his congregation.

WOODGATES

Woodgates to Cold Coates

Walk past house to go over stile by gate. Pass barn and walk along track to corner in wall. Cross field directly, keeping the brook on your left to go through gate. Follow left-hand fence, passing barn on right, to walk down and cross brook to go through gate. Follow right-hand fence and cross field to enter farmyard and on to roadway. Turn right, then left and walk up Collins Hill Lane to Cold Coates, the first farm on the right.

Cold Coates

Cold Coates is a modern farmhouse, but a closer look at its fabric will reveal some interesting features. Above the back doorway is a carved datestone of 1661, with the initials J.B.G. In the side wall of the barn can be found the steps of the

COLDCOATES

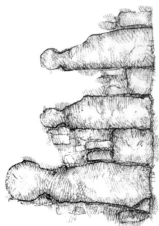

spiral staircase from the earlier, once thatched, farmstead. Below these stones is an old small trough dated 1842, with the initials W.M., and near the gate is an old corn weight, complete with Roman numerals.

The Parkinsons of Chipping lived here from the early 18th century, till Ralph Parkinson sold Cold Coates and went to reside at Daub Hall where he died in 1878, aged 66.

COLD COATES

Cold Coates to Chipping

Cross road and enter farmyard to go through gate opposite. Follow left-hand fence to go over stile and on, following left-hand fence to go over fence (there should be a stile here). Cross field on right diagonal keeping house to your left to go over fence (stile missing). Cross field on slight left diagonal following track to Clark House. Turn right and follow road to Chipping.

Fair Snape Well

Walk 2

Hidden under the old fire beacon

Approx. 3½, 7, 7½ or 13 miles.
Allow 2¼, 4, 4½ and 7 hours respectively.

O.S. maps SD 43/53, 44/54, PATHFINDER SERIES.
Lunch: Eccles Moss Post Office Cafe.
Start: Alston Arms, Longridge.

Folklore, legend, myth and fact combine to make this one of the most pleasing walks you will ever undertake. From tales of a mammoth cow to subterranean passages, from fireside insurrection and revolt to persecution, this ramble has it all, along with some of the finest countryside that Lancashire has to offer.

This walk again allows the traveller several combinations of walk apart from the main one: the north and south districts of Beacon Fell make up one or two short walks; and north-west and south-east of White Moss Gate make one or two more rambles. Whatever combination of walks you take satisfaction is guaranteed from start to finish. The main walk starts from the Alston Arms, Longridge.

Alston Arms to Dun Cow Rib & Ashes

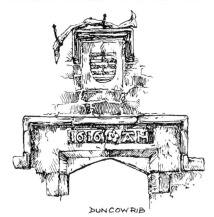

Walk up from the Alston Arms to turn left into Halfpenny Lane. Dun Cow Rib is down the lane on the right and Ashes is further on down a farm lane on the right.

DUN COW RIB

Dun Cow Rib Farm (Moor House)

This is a good type of the small stone-built 17th-century yeoman farmhouse. Of two storeys, it has low mullioned windows and a medieval latrine, set on corbles, built out from the east gable. Upon the doorhead are the initials of Adam Hoghton and the date 1616, together with the Hoghton arms on a shield. Over the shield fastened to the wall with iron bands is the rib of the Grimsargh Dun Cow.

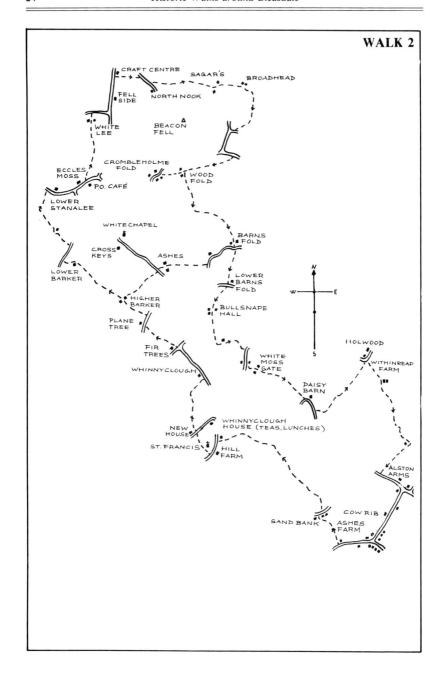

WALK 2

Local tradition has it that during the plague that reaped through Lancashire after the Civil Wars a gigantic dun cow appeared, and gave an almost unlimited supply of milk, which saved the local inhabitants from death wrought by the pestilence. One day an old witch, with a view to obtain from the beast more than the number of pailfulls, milked the cow with a colander, which, of course, never became full, as the precious liquid passed through the orifices into a vessel below. The story goes on to say that the cow died of grief at detecting the imposture, or from sheer exhaustion. A locality is still pointed out, named 'Cow Hill', where the huge bones of the said cow were disinterred by local people who, regretting its loss, wished to preserve some part for a memorial, or good luck.

It is true that a great pestilence hit Lancashire during the late 1640s. Non payment of the militia and several crop failures aggravated the situation. As to the appearance of the great cow, could it be one of those large heifers of Craven wandered lost from the Bowland Fells? Needless to say that the bone in question is not a cow's rib, but probably part of a whale or an ancient auroch from Bronze Age times. The twisted remains we see today were once much larger. Over the years people have chipped fragments off in the hope that some luck would rub off on them. Outside Grimsargh Hall there is another Dun Cow rib which is in good condition and nearly six foot in length.

Ashes Farm

Ashes Farm stands in a secluded spot just off Halfpenny Lane, so near to Longridge yet, in its tree-shrouded rural position, so far away. The house is a delight of gables and mullioned windows, all fairing well for its three hundred

years. Above the sheltered front doorway is a datestone of 1683 along with the initials W.C.A.

ASHES

Halfpenny Lane to the Hill Chapel

Walk on down the lane and turn right at the roadway. Walk on to turn right by Water Works building. Walk up the lane to Sandy Bank Farm. Walk through farmyard to road. Turn right and cross the road to go over stile. Cross field on a right diagonal to far corner to go through gap in hedge to go over stile on right. Follow left-hand hedge to go over stile and follow left-hand fence to go over stile. Cross field on a slight right diagonal to go over footbridge in hedge. Cross field directly to go over next footbridge. Follow left-hand fence to corner in fence. Cross field on a left diagonal to go over footbridge and stile in hedgerow on left. Follow right-hand hedgerow to bear left to go over footbridge to go over stile opposite.

Walk directly up to go left round the pond to go over stile opposite. Follow left-hand hedgerow to go left over stile in hedgerow, to go right and through a gate opposite. Cross field on a right diagonal to farm to pass through gate onto road. Walk left along the road past house on left to walk up first lane on right to the Hill Chapel.

The Hill, St. Francis Chapel

In 1600 the Hill was the residence of a family named Beesley. Francis Beesley was fined for recusancy between 1591 and 1607. His brother George, ordained at Rheims in 1587, was sent on the English Mission in 1588. He was captured after

THE HILL CHAPEL

about two years and, though tortured to make him reveal the names of his host, he would tell nothing and was at last executed for his priesthood in Fleet Street, London, in 1591.

Hill Chapel, St. Francis R.C., was established in 1687; the present church is of 1802 with a facade of 1835. It has arched windows and an open bell turret. In 1987 the church celebrated its Tercentenary, a good thing having survived those dark 16th- and 17th-century times giving the eternal light of hope to the many Catholic families in the area.

Hill Chapel to New House

Looking at the front of the church turn left and walk on to go through gate, then over stile on left. Follow right-hand line of trees to cross brook. Follow right-hand fence to go over stile onto road. New House is on the left (The Cottage — lunch and teas — is down the road on the right).

New House & Whinnyclough House

New House is an attractive Georgian house which has a datestone of 1733 with the initials I.T.M. Down the road can be found the old Whinnyclough House, now

NEW HOUSE

WHINNYCLOUGH
HOUSE

known as 'The Cottage'. We recommend that at some time you visit The Cottage to sample the excellent fare it has on offer; lunches and dinners, high teas and afternoon teas are served in most inviting surroundings. The house frontage and gardens are a joy to the eye. Above the doorway is a datestone of 1771 and the initials J.I.M.

YE HORNS INN

WHINNYCLOUGH
BRIDGE

New House to Whinnyclough

Walk back to stile and go over stile opposite. Follow left-hand hedge to go over stile on right. Cross field on a slight right diagonal to go over stile. Cross the field on a right diagonal to go through gate. Follow brook to enter Whinnyclough through gate.

Whinnyclough

Whinnyclough was part of the Hoghton estate in around 1569. The present house was built by the Cawthornes in 1706. Their coat of arms and the date are carved on a tablet above the front doorway.

The barn, which was built in times when labour was cheap, is a rare gem indeed. Proud finials surmount the gables and solid oak timbers support the roof. But what makes this barn so special is that a farm worker's cottage is built into the west end. Small mullioned windows peer out from behind more recent structures. The early 17th-century doorway is to be found complete, the doorhead of which has the date

WHINNYCLOUGH

1639 along with the initials of Robert and Alice Bamber. Edward Bamber of Whinnyclough travelled to France to join the Roman Catholic institution at Douay. Having become a priest, he returned on the English Mission to be thrice apprehended for his beliefs. He was finally executed at Lancaster in 1646.

Whinnyclough to Fir Trees

Leaving the house walk past the front of the barn to road-way. Turn left and walk up to junction. Fir Trees is the first house on the left.

WHINNYCLOUGH   WHINNYCLOUGH, 1639

Fir Trees & Isles Field Farm

Fir Trees displays a finely carved early 18th-century doorhead, but no date or initials occur. Isles Field Farm, just down the road, also has a good period doorhead and this time we have a date, 1709, with the initials W.H.M.

FIR TREES

Fir Trees to Higher Barker

Go through the gate on the right of the house, through next gate and over a stile on left. Cross field on a slight left diagonal keeping pond on your left to go over footbridge by a group of trees. Follow right-hand hedge to go over next footbridge. Cross field on a slight left diagonal to go through gate onto roadway. Turn right and walk on to turn left by next lane. Follow farm lane to Higher Barker.

Higher Barker

Higher Barker

In the 1450s, Barker in Goosnargh was a portion of the estates of Richard Clifton of Clifton. Today, as then, it consisted only of a few farmsteads, Higher Barker being one. The present edifice is a modern farmhouse, but built into a wall at the rear of the house is a datestone of 1704 with the initials I.G.I.

What follows now is a diversion over to Ashes and Barns Fold intended for those choosing one of the shorter variants of the walk. A brief history of Ashes is also included.

Higher Barker to Ashes

Looking at the farmhouse front from gateway, go right through gate and cross brook. Follow brook up to go over stile to cross the brook. Follow right-hand fence to go over stile. Cross the field on a slight left diagonal to go over stile. Follow left-hand line of trees to go over stile onto roadway. Cross the road and walk up the farm lane to Ashes.

The Ashes

ASHES

Ashes stands in a secluded situation off Church Lane but, apart from the doorway, it is of little interest, having been wholly modernised. Traces of a moat are still to be seen and in one of the walls, which is from four to six feet thick, are cavities, said to be hiding places for local Catholics. The doorhead is splendid, depicting an angel of the Lord with spreading wings.

The house was originally the residence of the Threlfall family, having been here from around 1311. Edmund Threlfall of the Ashes died in 1617, leaving the estate to his son John then aged twelve. Edmund had suffered the sequestration of two thirds of his estate for his Catholic faith in 1607. John died in 1625 and it was another son, Cuthbert, who inherited the Ashes, only to have it sequestered for 'delinquency' under the Commonwealth and forfeited in 1653. Cuthbert's son Edmund was a Jacobite and was killed by a party of soldiers sent to arrest him in 1690. Edmund was succeeded by his brother Cuthbert who was described as a 'papist' when he registered his estate in 1717. A brother, John, who was in possession soon afterwards, was to sell the house in the later part of the century.

Ashes to Barns Fold

Walk on through the farmyard to go over the fence into the field. Walk up, then follow the left-hand fence to go over stile. Walk directly on to the roadway. Turn left and walk up to Barns Fold.

Higher Barker to Lower Barker

Walk straight through the farmyard to the right corner of the last farmbuilding. Cross the field on a slight left diagonal to far corner to go over stile by a pond. Cross field on a left diagonal to go over stile and cross next field directly to go over stile. Cross field bearing left to the right of a group of farmbuildings to go through a gate between two sheds by a brook. Walk into Lower Barker farmyard.

Lower Barker

In around 1675, Lower Barker was the residence of the Lords of the Manor of Goosnargh. John Warren, who in 1674 procured the royal Charter for holding two fairs at Inglewhite in his tithing, lived at Lower Barker. The old house is unrecognisable today, being much altered and covered in stucco. Over the main door of the barn is a datestone of 1651, with the initials H.C. (Clifton of Clifton).

LOWER BARKER

Lower Barker to Lower Stanalee & Eccles Moss P.O. Cafe

Follow farm lane onto road, right, and walk along the road to take the farm lane on the left. Walk on to pass through Lower Trotter Farm to go through left-hand gate. Follow right-hand hedgerow to go over stile on left and on, following right-hand hedge, to a big tree stump. Go over the fence and follow left-hand hedge to go over stile on left near pond. Cross the field on a right diagonal to go through gateway onto road. Turn right and walk on to Lower Stanalee on the left. Walk on down the road to Eccles Moss.

Lower Stanalee & Eccles Moss

LOWER STANALEE

Lower Stanalee could easily be dismissed by the casual eye. But a closer look would reveal a beautiful leaded and dated rainwater head. It bears the date 1746, with cherubs and a face worked onto the head itself. In the front garden is a collection of farm troughs and the weight of an old cheese press, but the real treasure here lies in the field beyond. The barn at Lower Stanalee is a timber-built structure of three great oaken crucks which is crowned by a roof of thatch (now covered with metal sheeting for protection). A cruck-built thatched building in this part of Lancashire is very rare indeed. What a little gem!

Eccles Moss Post Office Cafe makes a good lunch stop and a shop is on hand for cheese, cooked meats and bread for those wanting to make their own sandwiches.

Cruck Barn, Lower Stanalee.

Eccles Moss to White Lee

Go over stile in hedge opposite post office, and walk through trees to go over stile in fence on right. Cross the field on a left diagonal to go through gateway. Cross field on a left diagonal to pass through gate in far corner. Follow left-hand line of trees to go through gate onto farm lane. Follow lane up to enter White Lee by gate.

White Lee

WHITE LEE

White Lee, part of the Catterall estate in Threlfall, was sold as one third of a manor in 1591 to James Kighley by Gervaise Strechland. The last of the Kighleys of White Lee joined the Jacobite Rebellion of 1715 and later left the country in fear for his life. The Kighleys were one of many families in the district who adhered to the Roman Catholic faith. In fact, at the south end of the house, there once stood an early 18th-century Roman Catholic chapel until it was pulled down in the 1830s.

Upon an old gatepost are carved the initials I-M.K, with the date 1694 (Hugh and Mary Kighley?).

By the side of the farmyard gate stands a once very sturdy horse-drawn cart; it must be well over a hundred years old and is not yet beyond restoration.

White Lee

White Lee to Fell Side

Walk past the house and follow farm lane onto road. Turn right and walk on to turn left at T-junction. Walk 250m to find Fell Side Farm on your right.

Fell Side

Resting on the western slopes of Beacon Fell is the solid and substantial farmhouse of Fellside. Its ancient mullions have been removed, but their positions are still discernible. The doorhead is dated 1707 with the initials W.W.A.

FELLSIDE

Beacon Fell is so named after the ancient fire beacon that once dominated its summit. Beacons are also known to have existed on Pendle and Longridge Fell. These 'land lighthouses' have been used from Roman times to guide the traveller through difficult countryside or to warn of some event or danger.

Fell Side to Broadhead

Follow the road to turn right passing front of Craft Centre shop to go over stile by a brook. Follow brook to go over next stile. Follow right-hand hedgerow to go over footbridge. Cross field directly to go over footbridge onto road. Turn right and walk on to go over stile on left by gate. Cross field on a slight right diagonal to go over stile. Cross field directly to go through gate and cross next field directly to go over stile. Cross brook and follow old field boundary on, over stream, and on across field to go over stile by farm lane. Follow lane to go over stile by gate onto drive. Turn left and walk down to house entrance gates. Right, following left-hand track into Sagar's. Follow the track to go left at fork and on, to enter Broadhead through gate.

BROADHEAD

Broadhead

Broadhead, once known as Dowhey, was the home of Robert Parkinson in 1619. Above the front doorway is a dated tablet of 1770 with the initials A.P.

Broadhead to Woodfold

Go back to the gate and go through gate opposite. Follow track up to go through gate on left. Walk up the trackway, through two gateways, on up to corner in right-hand fence. Walk up the field on a right diagonal to far corner to go over stile onto road. Turn right, then left, and walk down the road to go left at bottom. Walk on to go through gateway on right. Walk across the field on a right diagonal towards a group of trees to go over a stile in fence to the right of the trees. Cross field directly to go through gateway in wall. Cross the field on a slight left diagonal to go through gate. Follow right-hand wall, then fence, to go through gate. Follow farm lane to Woodfold.

Woodfold & Crombleholme Fold

Woodfold stands in an elevated position above the farmyard amid rather well laid out gardens. The doorhead here is finely cut and in fine condition for its date of 1696. Above the date are the initials T.B.E. Sadly, most of the mullions have been removed leaving the frontage rather bland and meaningless.

Crombleholme Fold stands just down the lane from Woodfold and consists of two farmsteads. Standing in one of the gardens is a relic of the ancient Crombleholme family (from Ribchester) in the form of a sun-dial, bearing the initials R.C. I.C. and the date 1697. In 1574 one Richard Crombleholme from here was arrested as a papist along with George Hothersall and four youths called Worthington. They were all imprisoned for their faith in the Tower of London.

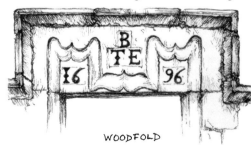

WOODFOLD

Crombleholme Fold

Crombleholme Fold

A short walk down the road will bring you to the tiny hamlet of Whitechapel — a pub, a school, a church and some weavers' cottages. But the Cross Keys Inn and the church are well worth a visit.

St. James, Whitechapel

St. James Church is also known by the name Threlfall Chapel, as it is believed that it was originally erected as a private chapel for the Threlfalls of Ashes during Elizabethan times. Records show that divine service was held here in 1581 and the windows on the west wall belong to this period. A story is also told of Alexander

Hoghton removing the bell in 1581 with a promise to replace it when required to do so. In 1728 an application was made to Sir Henry de Hoghton for the bell, who, instead of returning it, stated that "Queen Elizabeth had given a bond to his ancestors for £50, which was not worth anything, and that he (being of Hoghton Tower) had no tenants in Goosnargh". He gave, however, 10s. for a new bell. The present church bears no date, but several of the pews are dated 1739. In 1820 a base of an ancient cross is recorded to have stood in the churchyard. We can find no sign of this today. Inside, the communion table and rails are worth looking at, being handsome and elaborately carved in oak by a former minister, Rev. T. Benn.

The village of Whitechapel used to be occupied by a colony of handloom weavers. They have long gone but their homes still survive. The Cross Keys Inn is also worth a visit, being one of the few traditional inns still to survive in Lancashire.

Woodfold to Barns Fold

Walk back up the lane to go through gateway on the right. Follow track, then left-hand hedgerow to go over stile. Follow left-hand fence to go over stile in corner. Follow right-hand fence to cross brook. Follow right-hand hedgerow to go over stile by a gate. Cross field on a right diagonal to go through gate to Barns Fold. Turn right through farmyard to dated white cottage.

Barns Fold

On entering Barns Fold from Woodfold the first house to be noticed is the newly converted barn and house. For many years the gable of the old house was slated and it was only when this was removed that a blocked mullioned window with a datestone above appeared. The date is 1706 with the initials A.H.A. The other house of note in the Fold is the white cottage, dated 1679 with the initials W.I.:N.E. The foundations of this building go back to 1554 and the well of this earlier house still exists beneath the present kitchen floor. Standing to the north of the cottage is what looks like a small farm out-building with a chimney at one end. This was once an old farm-worker's cottage, and it is difficult today to imagine a family living in such a place. The building opposite the cottage was originally the Smithy at Barns Fold, all going to show that this was once a busy place indeed.

Barns Fold to Bullsnape Hall

Walk down to roadway, turn right then right over bridge to go through left-hand gate. Follow right-hand hedge to corner and cross field directly to go over stile. Walk directly up to go over stile onto road. Turn right and pass through gate on left. Follow right-hand hedge to go through gate, then another gate on left. Cross field on right diagonal to go through gate between two outbuildings to enter Bullsnape Hall farmyard and walk round to the front of the house.

Bullsnape Hall (Manor)

In 1160 Bernardson, of Ailsi, became lord of the manor of Goosnargh and resided at Bullsnape Hall. In 1190 his son gave his lands to the Knights of St. John of Jerusalem. By 1244, Richard de Catterall and Adam de Catterall in 1397 held the manor of the Hospitallers. In 1515 Ralf Catterall, and his son John in 1517, held the same by a rent of 8s. In 1579 the whole estate was recorded to have been held by the Knights. The Catteralls appear to be the only manorial family resident within Goosnargh. The family had no male issue. On the partition the manor of Bullsnape became the residence of Thomas Procter in right of his wife Elizabeth, daughter of Thomas Catterall (1579).

The hall is a three-storey building, now used as a farmhouse. It was originally E-shaped in plan with wide end gables and a narrow middle one over the porch, which is the full height of the house. The building is now much modernised; the left wing has been pulled down, most windows have been replaced with new ones and the walls covered with stucco. An oak staircase with carved balustrade still remains and other evidence of the original building is visible in the interior. Remains of a moat, which have now disappeared, could be seen up to 1856.

Bullsnape Hall to Alston Arms

With your back to the front of the house walk on to go over stile by gate. Follow left-hand fence/hedgerow to corner, and on, keeping the overhead lines on your right, over to two gates. Left, and walk down to go over stile. Walk on passing house to go over a bridge. Follow lane to the road. Turn right and walk on to take the second farm lane on left after first house. Follow lane to Wood Nook Farm.

Walk through farmyard, through gate, and on through farmyard to go over stile by gate on right and over to right-hand hedge. Follow hedge to corner and on across the field on a left diagonal to go through gate on left. Follow right-hand fence to go over stile. Follow left-hand fence, then track to go over stile by gate on left as track bends. Left, and walk up the road to go through second gate on left. Follow right-hand fence, past gateway, and on, over fence (should be a stile here), and on to go through gateway. Walk on to the right of the pond and on a slight right diagonal walk across the field, keeping the large hollow on your right, to go down and over footbridge. Walk up and follow right-hand fence/hedge to go over old gate by roadway. Go over the stile by gate on left. Walk on towards farm to go over footbridge. Walk up to enter Withinreap Farm by gate.

Walk on through farmyard to go through long gate and walk down to go through the next two gates. Cross field on a left diagonal to go over stile. Right, passing pond, to far corner to go over stile by gate. Follow left-hand hedge, through old gateposts, and on to go over stile by gate. Walk up track to farm lane. Turn right and walk down to go right around the front garden wall of house to go through gate. Follow left-hand hedge/fence on, over stile, and on over next stile onto roadway. Turn left and walk down to the Alston Arms.

Walk 3

Hidden in the Vale of the Loud

Approx. 8 miles. Allow 6 hours.

O.S. maps SD 44/54, 64/74 & 63/73 PATHFINDER SERIES.
Lunch: We recommend a diversion from Black Hall into Chipping to have lunch at the
Sun Inn. If the walk is started at Chipping, then the Derby Arms can be well
recommended.
Start: Derby Arms, Thornley with Wheatley

This walk takes us into a little known area in the Vale of the Loud which is often overlooked by the walker and visitor alike. The ramble is easy going and a pleasure to undertake and, though White Hill and Hesketh End are the major sites of interest, the others are notable and invite question. So enjoy your walk — you have a good day ahead of you.

The Derby Arms

The Derby Arms is an historic old coaching house that is the central focus of Thornley with Wheatley. The inn is run by the Walne family who have ancient and strong connections within the Chippingdale area, having farmed here for generations. The inn offers a fine selection of freshly prepared dishes using only the finest ingredients which are for the most part local produce. For you walkers we recommend the 'Chalk Board Specials' which give seasonal food at value for money prices; washed down with a bottle of vintage port, these should really set you up for the rest of the day.

THE DERBY ARMS

The inn takes its name from Sir Edward Stanley of Bickerstaffe, whose mother Elizabeth Patten resided at Thornley Hall in the early 17th century.

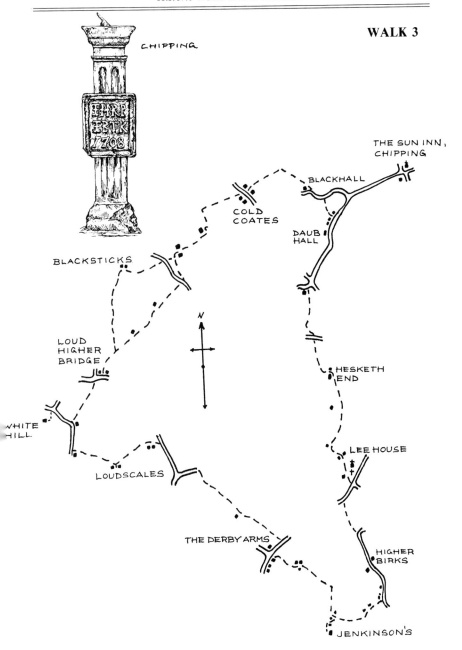

WALK 3

CHIPPING

THE SUN INN,
CHIPPING

BLACKHALL

COLD
COATES

DAUB
HALL

BLACKSTICKS

LOUD
HIGHER
BRIDGE

HESKETH
END

WHITE
HILL

LEE HOUSE

LOUDSCALES

THE DERBY ARMS

HIGHER
BIRKS

JENKINSON'S

Derby Arms to Loudscales

On leaving the pub, turn left and walk along the road to turn left by the next lane leading to Blackmoss Country House Hotel. Walk past the hotel and follow trackway on to junction, left and walk down to roadway. Turn right and walk on to turn left by the first house to go through a gate. Walk straight through the farmyard to go through a small gate, then a gate on the right opposite. Follow right-hand fence to go over stile, left to corner and under fence to cross field directly to enter Loudscales by gates on right.

Loudscales

The present farmstead was built in 1856 upon the site of an earlier house of 1666. An old doorhead above the front door recalls this date, along with the initials T.A.K., the initials of Thomas Knowles.

An interesting story is told locally of one of the former owners of Loudscales who staked the farm in a card game. He lost holding an ace, a two and a three and was heard to exclaim "Ace, deuce and tray, Loudscales, go thi way".

Loudscales has its origins in the 10th century, its name coming from an old Norwegian place-name meaning 'the huts by the River Loud'.

Loudscales to White Hill

Return to the bridge to go through a gate by a shed. Follow brook up to junction of streams. Follow left-hand brook up to go over slab bridge. Cross field on left diagonal to corner of fences facing front of white cottages. Go over fence (should be a stile here). Cross field to right of house, through gate onto road. Turn right and walk up the road to White Hill, the first house on the left. Walk up the farm lane to house (good eggs for sale here).

White Hill

White Hill was once the seat of a branch of the Hesketh family, who, being Roman Catholics, took the King's side during the Civil Wars. This action led them to have their estate sequestered. The family also took a part in the Jacobite Rebellion of 1715, which led to forfeiture of the estate. This branch of the Hesketh family were known as Aughton, their arms being engraved on a stone above the front door.

White Hill

Local tradition obtains that there formerly existed a secret underground passage from White Hill to Ashes at Whitechapel — the Heskeths/ Aughtons of White Hill and the Threlfalls of Ashes inter-married in the 17th century, both families were strong and devout Catholics and were forever engaged in plots against the Protestant government.

In the late 17th century, Cuthbert Hesketh gave financial aid and encouragement for a chapel to be built at White Hill on condition that masses would be said for the poor of Goosnargh and Chipping. The original chapel was destroyed, which led to it being re-established on its present site below Horns, but taking the 'Hill' name with it as a reminder of the former place of worship.

The Franciscans worked from White Hill for over 147 years. In 1746 Father Germanus Helme from White Hill was taken to Lancaster Castle, where he was to become the last priest to die for the Catholic faith in England.

White Hill to Cold Coates

Follow the road back to go over stile in hedge on left at side of corner house. Follow right-hand fence to cross a brook. Walk straight up to go over stile. Follow hedgerow up to go over stile onto road. Turn right, then left up driveway passing side of white house to go through a gate. Follow right-hand hedge, over a stile and on, to go over a footbridge on left and up to go over fence stile. Follow left-hand fence to go through a gate ahead. Follow left-hand fence to go over a stile in a wall, then through a gate on right. Turn left and walk past a shed to go over a stile by gate. Cross field directly to go over stile. Cross field directly to go through a gate. Follow left-hand hedgerow to go through a gate on left onto farm trackway. Follow track right to go over a fence (a stile missing here) by a stone wall where the track bends. Cross field directly to go through gate on left of stream onto road. Turn right, then left, to follow the lane up into farmyard. Straight on, through fence-gate and on up, over blocked gateway, and on to go through gate on right. Follow left-hand fence, then hedge, to go over stile. Cross brook and walk up to go through gap in hedgerow. Walk up to right of farm entrance. Over stile and on to corner then over to follow left-hand hedgerow to go over stile by gate. Right, walking up towards Parlick to follow old trackway to gate (do not go over stile). Turn right and follow left-hand fence on to go over stile. Cross field directly to go through a gate. Cross field directly to go over fence stile. Cross field on a slight right diagonal to far corner to go through gate onto road. Cold Coates farmhouse is on the right.

Cold Coates

See Walk No. 1 for information on this farmstead.

Cold Coates to Black Hall

Cross road and walk through farmyard to go through gate. Follow left-hand fence to go over stile. Follow left-hand fence on to corner, turn right and walk directly down to find old lane in group of trees. Follow lane down onto road. Turn left into Black Hall.

Black Hall

During the 14th century the Hoghtons held Black Hall as half the manor of Chipping. With the Shireburns of Wolf Hall, they held rival manorial courts in the village. By 1556 Black Hall was regarded as the manor house of Chipping and by the early 17th century the Hoghtons held the only village court, with the Shireburns in attendance.

The house went on to become the seat of the Midgehall family. Edward Midgehall took the King's side in the Civil Wars. His estates were sequestered and ultimately sold for his 'delinquency' by the Parliament in around 1660. His family turned to Protestantism in 1662 and regained Black Hall, which continued in the family until 1807. The present house was built by John and Margaret Parkinson in 1786.

Of the old Black Hall few parts remain — an open fireplace in the kitchen and a dining table of carved oak bearing the initials A.M. 1630. Some parts of the original building have now been converted into stables.

Black Hall to Daub Hall

Go through gate opposite Black Hall farmhouse and follow left-hand hedgerow to go over stile. Follow old trackway to go through a gate onto road. Turn right and walk down the road to Daub Hall.

Daub Hall

Daub Hall is first recorded in 1334, when John, son of William de Dubhill, was registered as living in the parish of Chipping. The place-name comes from the Old English 'dub', meaning pool, or, in this case, ditch.

The Singleton family dwelt here from 1578 to 1682 when the hall passed to the Parkinson family. From 1725 to 1736, Peter Walkden, a Manchester diarist and incumbent of the Hesketh Lane Independent Chapel from 1711 to 1738, had lease of the property from John Parkinson. Whilst in Chipping, Walkden wrote a drama entitled *Kelly, Or the Modern Reformer*, based on behaviour he observed among those who frequented the Dog

Daub Hall

Daub Hall

and Partridge, (formerly the 'Green Man' and 'Cliviger House' in the 17th century). The play is a gem in its own right and ought to be performed again.

An old doorhead is built into the right side of the house front. It is dated 1707 with the initials L.W., being those of Lawrence Wall of Preston who built the house. His son married a Mary Parkinson. Signs of the house's older mullioned windows can still be made out, along with the massive weight of a cheese press.

DAUB HALL

Daub Hall to Hesketh End

Walk down Parsonage Lane, over the crossroads, to go over hedge stile on the left in front of Astley House. Cross the field to go over fence stile on the right. Cross the field by the edge of the marshy ground and follow banking down to stream. Follow stream down to go over stile in fence and up, over flat bridge, through gate to roadway. Pass through gateway opposite and follow left-hand hedgerow to go through second gate on left. Walk down to go over stile on left by the fodder trough in the hedge to the right of the farm. Walk on to the gateway then walk up the track, through the farmyard, to the front of Hesketh End.

Hesketh End

Richard Alston built this house on land purchased from Gabrial Hesketh, a recent landowner in the district. The building comes to note by the fact that it has a running frieze of two line panels forming a band of lettering around the house. The inscriptions contained in the frieze refer to events in English history from the Roman period to the Battle of Flodden Field in 1513. In 1907 the house was thoroughly restored after a fire, the main front being largely reconstructed. The original building probably extended further. The inscription runs across the front wall in double lines, carved on six separate stones.

HESKETH END

Hesketh End

The wording on each stone is complete in itself, except in the last two stones, and is as follows:

1. BRUTUS ERECTUS LON DINV ANTE CHRIST 1108
2. CESAR CONQVERT AN GLIA ANTE CHRIST 58
3. SAXONII CONQVERT ANGLIA ANNO DON 447 EBISCOPAT IB
4. DANII CONQVERT A NGLIA ANNO DON 1018
5. ANGLIA IN CO M**SIVE**SHIRI
6. ANGL** RECEP* FIDM AD 179

This is continued on four stones along the return of the west wing:

1. ANNO DOMI 1591 ELIS REGI REGNO ANNI ETATIS NOSTRE
2. ROBART ALSTUN 25 RIC ALSTUN IVNIOR 5
3. A CREACIONE MUNDI 5553 A CONQVES TO ANGLIE 524 DEUM TIME REGEM HONOR
4. RESPICE FINEM ET NVNQV AM PECCABIS PROXIMUM AMA

To the left of this last stone is another stone with the name of RICHARDE ALSTUN 53. On the main south front are other inscribed stones, one with the sacred monogram between two crosses, another with the fragment RIC AULSTU, and a third ALSTUN HATH INHERITED HERE IB 18 YER. The west wall retains its old rough stone walling unrestored. The chimney has two gargoyles in the angles. There is an inscribed stone in the main bedroom — FEAR GOD AND LOVE THE RIGHT.

What a sense of wonder the local peasantry must have felt when looking upon the house of Richard Alston, a ray of illumination in their dark. rustic lives.

Hesketh End to Lee House

Walk down the lane to go over stile in hedge on right. Cross the field on a left diagonal to corner fence, then walk on to go over footbridge and onto the road. Go over stile on right opposite and cross the field directly to pass through far gate. Follow left-hand hedge up to go through gate. Left, and follow farm track through farmyards to main road. Lee House is down the road on the left.

St. William, Lee House

The Roman Catholic church of St. William of York, also known as Lee House Chapel, is a good example of a post-Reformation chapel. The chapel was founded by Thomas Eccles of Thornley in 1738 and was originally housed in the present priest's house. A secret room built into the eaves of the building can still be located. This house has a datestone of 1677, with the initials T.A., and at the rear a few old mullioned windows still exist.

Thomas Eccles gave the house to the English Franciscans, and on their approaching extinction in 1826 the secular clergy took charge for a time. After 1859 it was served by the English Benedictines, whose gravestones can be found in the churchyard.

Hidden in the undergrowth of the churchyard is the base of the old Wheatley Lane Cross which once stood near to Wheatley Brook.

Lee House Thornley with Wheatley

Lee House to Higher Burks

Walk back along the road, down the dip and up to go over stile on left after the last 'hazzard' post. Cross the field on a slight right diagonal to go over ford. Follow right-hand hedgeway up to go over stile onto road. Walk up the road to Higher Burks.

Higher Burks

The farmer at Higher Burks informs me that the farmhouse was once an inn, known as 'The Dog and Pheasant'. The house dates back to 1663, and an inventory of the house's contents then does include more household goods and equipment than would be found in the average house of this type in those times. An inn, offering food and shelter, would account for this excess.

The front of the house is very grand, looking out over the Bowland Fells. It is Georgian and symmetrical in design; only at the rear can one see signs of the earlier building. The low mullioned windows are wholly original, but the tall stair-well window is a composite of re-used mullions. On the roadside, near the rear, stands an old horse mounting block — again suggesting its former status as an inn.

At the bottom of the front garden, built into the wall, is an old lime kiln. Before firing the limestone the front would be bricked up. A close inspection will reveal traces of fired lime upon all the stonework and the remains of the back flue. In the garden to the west of the house can be found the paved stones of a Donkey Walk — a shaft ran from this into the building on the end of the house which turned the stones to grind the fired lime into powder. The grindstones are still in existence, stored in one of the buildings adjoining the house. What with fine ales and bags of lime, the original owner must have been quite an entrepreneur.

The barn belonging to Higher Burks retains a single cruck 'A' frame mounted upon large stones. It is one of the few cruck built structures in the district.

Higher Burks to Jenkinsons Farm

Walk up the road to go over wall stile after second house on right. Follow left-hand wall down to go over wall stile. Through the conifers to go over wall stile to Hill Top Cottages (J.W.A. 1855).

HILL TOP COTTAGES

Walk past the front of cottages and over stile by gate. Through next gate, past front of house and over cattle-grid. Then right to go over stile in bottom corner. Follow right-hand fence to go over

JENKINSON'S

wall stile. Follow hedgerow down to go through gate, past the cottage to right of barn. Through the gate on left and cross the field on a left diagonal to pass through gate at rear of Jenkinsons Farm.

Jenkinsons Farm

This area between Hill Top Cottages and Jenkinsons Farm gives the appearance that time has stood still at this little corner end of the fell. An old fashioned quaintness exists here that is hard to find elsewhere. Farmbuildings huddle around tiny homesteads, as though providing a protective cloak from the intrusions of modern society.

Jenkinsons, dated 1726 with the initials R.A., truly recalls the former rural age — hard work from daybreak to moonrise, the smell of the animals and the good earth, calloused hands and bent knees, long skirts and iron shod clogs, hoof-falls on the cobbles and the swill and clang of milk churns. A far harder age, but one nearer to nature and, perhaps, to reality.

Jenkinsons

Jenkinsons to Derby Arms

Go back through gate and over field, through gate and up past barn and cottage to go back through gate. Left, down through gate and gate opposite to follow right-hand hedge around corner and on to pass through stone-slab stile. Cross field on left diagonal to go through gateway onto farm lane. Left, following lane through Little Town to the roadway. Turn left and walk up to the Derby Arms.

The hills above Baron Agmund's headland

Approx. 13 miles. Allow 7 hours.

O.S. map SD 44/54 PATHFINDER SERIES
We advise a packed lunch and flask on this walk, the only possible lunch spot being
the Post Office Cafe at Bleasdale.
Start: Brock, by the river.

A thousand years ago the lands covered by this walk were peopled by Scandinavians and British Celts whose joint lineage form the ancestral backbone of Lancastrians. If Halfdan, Athulf, Agmund, and later Anlaf had won some of those early battles with the English, Norse may have been a common form of spoken language in Britain today. The Celts are remembered through many river names and in certain forms of place-names. The homes of the Norwegians — the longhouse — are recalled in names such as Landskill and Loudscales. The walk takes us through their former landscape, over hills and along riverbanks, recalling places of interest along the way that hark back to a more rural and pastoral age.

Brock to Matshead

Walk to the right corner of a white building on the right of the petrol station. Follow the lane to cross the railway via two gates and on, to walk under the motorway to follow lane past a footbridge (do not go over) to enter Matshead by gate.

Matshead

The house presents a symmetrical frontage of cross-windows, the whole having been rebuilt some ten years ago due to the earlier building having no foundations. The decorated doorhead bears the date 1703, with the initials R.M. Around the

MATSHEAD

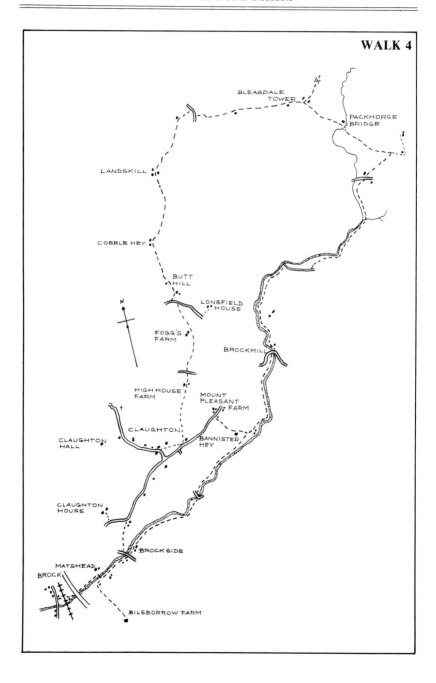

WALK 4

corner of the frontage is an older datestone built into the wall. It bears the initials H.B.A.B.E.B. 1618 W., being those of the Barton family.

In 1403 Matshead was held from the King by the Hollands of Denton. Hugh Barton purchased the house and some lane from Edward Holland in 1564. The Bartons resided here until the mid 17th century, when they were succeeded by the Whiteheads of Garstang, one of whom raised a company of soldiers for the Parliament in 1643.

Across the river are to be found the ruins of Matshead Paper Mill. Ivy and other creepers have now covered this early industrial enterprise, giving it a romantic beauty that it originally never possessed. Further up the lane stands Trout Row Cottage with its strangely designed roof. This covers the original thatched roof of an early 18th-century date. It has quite surprised me to find so large a number of thatched dwellings in the district, some of which we shall be visiting today.

Matshead to Claughton House

Walk back to the footbridge and cross the brook. Follow the trackway up to the road (the remains of the old Matshead Paper Mill are on the right as you cross the footbridge and Trout Row Cottage, dated 1737, is thatched). Turn left and walk over the bridge and past the petrol station to go over stile in hedge on the right. Follow left-hand hedge to go through gate to walk through farmyard onto road. Turn left and walk on to turn right up the driveway to Claughton House.

Claughton House

Claughton House has a late 17th-century facade, but above a rear doorway is a lintel of 1573 with the initials R.W. With the heavily studded door, it all lends to make a very strong, pleasing picture. The 16th-century lintel must be from an earlier building on the site.

Just north west of Claughton House, on Lodge Road, is the site of a Viking burial place. Practical evidence of Norse settlement in the area was found in 1882, when, during a road construction at Claughton Hall estate, a small mound of sand was cut through. Between two and three feet below the surface the workmen discovered four iron objects — an axe-head, a hammer head, a spear head and a sword hilt, grip and pommel with a few inches of blade. Among the implements were ornaments with patterns of Scandinavian style — a pair of tortoise bronze brooches joined together forming a box which contained two beads, a flat silver brooch and a molar tooth. Together with these finds were a pottery vessel that is said to have contained a cremation and a perforated stone axe-hammer. The latter was of Bronze Age origin, being just as practical a tool to the Viking who found it as it had been to its original owner.

Apart from several illustrations, the iron-work along with the urn and its contents are lost to the record. The three brooches, two beads and the stone axe-hammer are now in the possession of Mr. M. Fitzherbert Brockholes at Claughton Hall.

The existence of the urn cremation and the axe-hammer have led some to conclude that the Viking burial had taken place in an earlier Bronze Age barrow, which may or may not be the case. Viking cremation and urn burials are rare; however, at nearby Inskip, a Viking burial was accompanied by a pottery vessel. The axe-hammer, more strictly a 'battle-axe', is of a common northern type found with cremations, perhaps used as a maul to pound the charred bones for insertion in the urn. What does confound the issue is that the total finds were said to have been contained in a wooden box, the nature of which must remain a matter of conjecture.

It is interesting to note here that, in 1899, a rougher type of stone axe was found in drainage operations half a mile north of the above site, although the two finds probably have no connection.

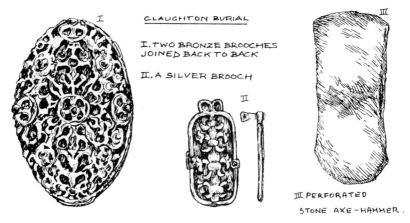

CLAUGHTON BURIAL

I. TWO BRONZE BROOCHES JOINED BACK TO BACK

II. A SILVER BROOCH

III. PERFORATED STONE AXE-HAMMER.

Claughton House to St. Thomas Church

Walk back to the road, turn left and walk on 1 km to turn left. Walk past the school and post office to find the church on the right.

Claughton

Claughton, pronounced Clighton, is mentioned in the Domesday Survey as the Old Norse settlement of 'Clactune' — hamlet near the small hillock. A hamlet is what it remains today, with its hall, church, school and a few cottages and farmsteads, some of which still have steeply-pitched thatched roofs and cruck constructions. The picture above shows one such cottage — Duckworth Hall

Farm. The Church of St. Thomas was built in 1792, being enlarged and decorated internally in 1835. The font bears the date 1699, and a medieval chalice brought from Mains Hall is preserved and in use here. The vestment chest and a small oak tabernacle which belonged to the Venerable Thomas Whitaker, who had ministered in the district and was executed at Lancaster in 1646, are also preserved.

St. Thomas Church to High House Farm

Follow the lane back to go left at fork to go up trackway, through gateway, then through gateway opposite (notice the cottage on the left with the mullioned windows; this was once thatched). Follow left-hand wall, then right-hand hedge to go over a stile on the right

onto the roadway. Turn left, then left again up the farm track to pass thatched house and follow track up to go over stile by gate on the left. Walk up the field following right-hand hedgerow to go over stile. Cross field on a left diagonal to corner onto farm lane. Walk up the lane to enter High House Farm through gate.

High House Farm

High House & Fogg's

High House is a solid looking 17th-century farmhouse, complete with its many mullioned windows. Fogg's farm has a datestone of 1730 with the initials I.G.M. and traces of the earlier mullioned windows can be made out in the stonework.

Fogg's Farm

High House Farm to Longfield House

Walk through the farmyard to go through gate by a barn. Walk on to go through a gate in hedge on the right. Cross field directly to go over stile onto road. Cross road to go through gate opposite. Follow left-hand line of trees to go over stile in corner. Follow overhead lines to go over stile and footbridge on the left. Follow telegraph line on to go over stile onto farm lane (Fogg's Farm is on the left). Cross the lane and walk directly up the field keeping overhead lines well to your right to go over stile by a gate onto road. Turn right and follow road to turn left by next driveway into Longfield House farm yard.

Longfield House. 1667.

Longfield House

Longfield House is an attractive 17th-century dwelling. Carved boldly upon the doorhead are the initials W.G.E. with a date of 1667. The farmstead stands on the high tongue of land between Bleasdale and Calder Vale, two areas of great contrast and beauty. Linking the two districts together, by way of Cobble Hey and Landskill, is the old trackway which now forms part of the modern roadway in front of Longfield House, Hobbs Lane — an interesting name that refers to the folk legend that a Hobgoblin resided in these parts. Names like this reflect a popular mythology, a belief in the supernatural world of dragons, elves, goblins, giants and dwarfs. Such creations of the popular imagination lived on long after the introduction of Christianity, and traces of these beliefs still exist today in names like Hobbs Lane.

Longfield House to Cobble Hey

Walk back to the stile and on to go right up Butt Hill farm lane. Walk up and follow round to the left, past Infield House, and on to Cobble Hey.

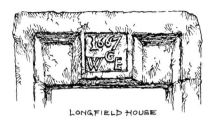

LONGFIELD HOUSE

COBBLE HEY

Cobble Hey

The ancient Hobbs Lane leads on through Butt Hill to enter the farmyard of Cobble Hey. With its traditional layout of farmbuildings, it affords the traveller a friendly and warming aspect. The farmhouse is of a 19th-century date, yet it still retains the doorhead of the former building. This is dated 1681 with the initials I.C.A.W. Notice also the garden gate posts — these stones are also from the fabric of the earlier house.

On the approach to Cobble Hey you will have noticed, over to the west, the very prominent Sullom Hill. Each time I view the hill I always think to myself, 'What a good position for a hill fort'. The position overlooks the Fylde and guards the upland dales and valleys of Bleasdale and the Loud, each a hive of Norse and earlier settlements. Who knows what momentous discoveries await the excavations of the modern archaeologist under this ancient turf?

The evidence for ancient settlement comes from various sources, principally place names. The name Sullom has its derivation in Old Norse, meaning 'pillar', or possibly British (Celtic) meaning 'sun'. Both meanings strongly hint that it could once have been an important focal point in the ancient past.

Many place names in the area give rise to speculation: the river Wyre is an old Celtic word meaning gore or blood; Skippol is Old Norse and refers to a harbour for longships; Dandy Birks is Hiberno Norse — Dunan's shieling or summer pasture; Catterall, again Old Norse, refers to a circular stone fort or tribal seat; Bilsborrow — the 'burh of the Bil', the settlement of the folk who once held sway between Whalley and Blackburn; Billington and Billinge are both sites of much Bronze Age activity; and the name Amounderness itself, refers to the Viking Baron Agmundr, who, as the *Anglo Saxon Chronicle* relates, led a great raid from these parts into Mercia in 911. For 937, the *Chronicle* records another great event which may well have been drawn to its bitter conclusion in the nearby surroundings. We may well be looking at the hill fort of Brunanburh or the hill of Weondun with its pagan temple that stood nearby. Who knows what secrets the near landscape holds? From all the evidence, it seems that this area is indeed steeped in ancient history.

Cobble Hey to Landskill

Walk past front of house, right, up through gate to follow trackway on, through next gateway to walk directly on and down to go through gate at stream. Follow right-hand fence and old trackway on and through gateway to go up farm track to Landskill.

Landskill

Landskill, as the place-name tells us, is the site of a Viking Longhouse perched high above Calder Vale. The house we see today was once the home of Francis and Martha Sherrington, whose initials and a date 1692 are recorded upon the ogee doorhead.

Landskill

In 1338 Roger de Brockholes purchased Landskill from Adam, son of Richard de Claughton. In 1590 an inquiry was made as to Thomas Brockhole's title to Landskill (then Langscales); it was said to be held for "superstitious uses", reference to the Catholic mass having been said there. Records also state that the base of an ancient cross once stood at Landskill.

The farmstead today comprises of two farms, the major property being a substantial Jacobean building with mullioned windows on both floors at the front, all leading to make a very pleasing picture.

Landskill to Packhorse Bridge

Walk back towards first house and on between sheds to go left up the lane. Walk up to go through gateway on right and follow track up to go over stone wall stile on left. Cross field on a right diagonal towards farm, and on to farm lane. Walk up to the road. Turn right and walk along the road to go left into pine wood at opening in wall. Follow track, through gate into field and on to walk down the driveway to Bleasdale Tower and on down to Brooks packhorse bridge. (The views walking down the driveway are magnificent, showing the Bleasdale amphitheatre at its grandest).

Brooks Packhorse Bridge

The packhorse bridge and the old village of Coolan are described in Walk no. 1.

Packhorse Bridge to Bannister Hey

Follow the roadway on, passing a turning on left to Admarsh Church, to go through field-gate on right before the school comes into view. Cross the field on a right diagonal and on, following right-hand fence to go through Weavers farmyard (W.G. 1847) onto road. Turn right and walk a few paces to go up the banking and over a stile. Follow path along edge of wood finally to go over stile on left. Walk down and cross the footbridge to go over fence on right. Follow river down to go over fence (stile missing). Follow right-hand fence to go over stile. Follow path on, following the river, over  footbridges, following river (not the sandy path that goes up) to cross a small brook. Turn left and follow path up onto lane. Turn right and follow the lane down to meet the river. Turn left (do not go over the footbridge) and follow the path to enter a lane by a cottage (notice the datestone: W.W. 1721). Follow lane up and walk on to turn right by a gate. Follow path down to go over stile. Walk on,

Cottage at Brock Waterworks

following the river, to go through a gate and on to go over stile by a gate at the site of the old Brock Mill (the grindstones are in the garden on the left). Walk past the house and over the bridge. Turn left and follow the riverside path, on, past a footbridge (do not cross) and on, taking right hand track at fork. Follow track up to turn left into Bannister Hey farm.

Brock Mill

Above Brock Mill, near the Water Works, stands an old white-washed cottage dated 1721, with the initials W.W., alone, derelict and neglected at the water's edge.

Within the ruins of the old Brock Corn Mill can be found the original grindstones, standing serenely among the ivy-clad walls of this former industrious enterprise.

Today the old mill marks the starting point of a Nature Conservation nature trail. The bench-tables in the landscaped area across the bridge make an ideal resting point before the return leg home.

Mount Pleasant & Bannister Hey

Mount Pleasant farm has a date-tablet of 1826 with the initials of Thomas Fitzherbert Brockholes Esquire, who remodelled the house from the 17th-century original. The datestone of the earlier building can be found in the gable wall of the barn. This is dated 1683 with the initials R.M. Remains of the older mullioned windows can also be seen.

MOUNT PLEASANT FARM

MOUNT PLEASANT FARM

BANNISTER HEY

Opposite stands Little Bannister Hey, again one of the district's many thatched farmsteads. Bannister Hey itself has a datestone of 1707 with the initials of Lawrence Cottam, whose ancestor, Richard Cottam, had his lands sequestered for his recusancy under the Commonwealth. Only the central section of the house is of an early date, the rest being modern extensions.

Bannister Hey to Mount Pleasant Farm

Follow the lane onto road, turn right and walk on to turn left at the first driveway into Mount Pleasant farm.

Mount Pleasant to Brock Side

Follow the lane back to Bannister Hey and on down to go over a stile by gateway on the right. Follow left-hand hedge to go over footbridge and on, following river to go over stile and on to go over next stile. Cross field to go over stile by bridge onto road. Walk over the bridge and turn right to go over stile. Follow left-hand line of trees to go over stiles by gates. Follow right-hand hedge to go over stile. Walk on following an old trackway along the riverside to turn left into Brock Side farmyard.

BROCK SIDE

Brock Side

Currently under major restoration, the farmhouse displays a frontage of cross-windows and a doorhead dated 1733 along with the initials B.W.C. The final results of the work should be most rewarding.

Brock Side to Brock

Follow farmlane onto road. Cross road and follow the lane opposite to go over footbridge. Follow the lane to go under the motorway and on, to cross the railway to follow the lane to Brock.

BILSBORROW
HALL FARM

Bilsborrow Hall Farm

Just south of Matshead, at the bottom of an old trackway, stands Bilsborrow Hall Farm. Though it is greatly altered and modernised, it still displays its ancient doorhead.

BROCKMILL

Observe the Country Code:

Enjoy the countryside and respect its life and work.

Guard against all risk of fire.

Fasten all gates.

Keep your dogs under close control.

Keep to public paths across farmland.

Use gates and stiles to cross fences, hedges and walls.

Leave livestock, crops and machinery alone.

Take your litter home.

Help to keep all water clean.

Protect wild life, plants and trees.

Take special care on country roads.

Make no unnecessary noise.